Contents

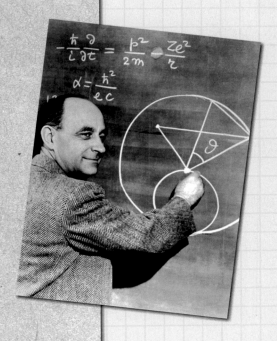

The Cold War

At the end of World War II, two nations emerged as the world's superpowers – the United States and the Soviet Union. They had both worked together to fight Germany and Japan during World War II. But between 1945 and 1991 they were extremely suspicious and hostile to one another. They both entered conflicts in other nations and threatened war. The period became known as the Cold War. It ended with the break-up of the Soviet Union into Russia and fourteen other nations.

US President Harry S. Truman (far left) sits with his most senior advisors in 1948. To his immediate right is Secretary of State, George C. Marshall, who developed a plan to help rebuild Europe after World War II.

During the Cold War, both the Soviet Union and the United States built strong alliances with other nations. Europe became effectively divided in two: the eastern European nations sided with the Soviet Union and most of western Europe was allied with the United States. The United States, Britain, West Germany and other nations formed the military alliance NATO (the North Atlantic Treaty Organisation) in 1949. The Soviet Union and its eastern European allies including Poland, Hungary, Czechoslovakia and Bulgaria responded with a similar alliance in 1955 known as the Warsaw Pact.

The Cold War began with both superpowers vying for influence in Europe, but they soon focused on other parts of the world, too. They offered huge amounts of aid to newly independent nations in Africa and Asia, sent troops to support struggling governments who were friendly to them and also plotted to replace leaders who were not. This lead to governments being overthrown in South America, Africa and Asia. Many fierce and bloody civil wars were fought around the world with arms and troops supplied by the superpowers. During the Cold War period, the United States

THE COLD WAR

Clive Gifford

WAYLAND

First published in 2009 by Wayland

Copyright © Wayland 2009

Wayland
338 Euston Road
London NW1 3BH

Wayland Australia
Level 17/207 Kent Street
Sydney NSW 2000

Editor: Julia Adams
Designer: Jason Anscomb (www.rawshock.co.uk)
Picture researcher: Diana Morris
Consultant: Dr Andrew Dilley
Proofreader and indexer: Sarah Doughty

British Library Cataloguing in Publication Data
Gifford, Clive.
   The who's who of the Cold War.
   1. Cold War--Biography--Juvenile literature.
   I. Title II. Cold War
   909.8'25'0922-dc22
ISBN 978 0 7502 5743 5

Picture acknowledgements:
Alinari/Topfoto: 4. AP/Topham: 7, 22, 23.
Classic Stock/Topfoto: 13. The Granger
Collection NYC/Topfoto: 17, 28. IIA/Topfoto:
20. Keystone/Getty Images: 25. Photri/Topfoto:
9. Private Collection: 7. RIA/Novosti/Alamy: 11.
RIA Novosti/Topfoto: front cover, 5, 10, 12, 14,
18, 24, 26, 27, 30. RKO/Kobal Collection: 29.
David Rubinger/Corbis: 21. Time Life Pictures/
Eupra/Getty Images: 16. Topfoto: 8, 15, 30.
Ullsteinbild/Topfoto: 19.

Printed in China

Wayland is a division of Hachette Children's
Books, an Hachette UK company.

www.hachette.co.uk

The arms race

During the Cold War, there was a large build-up of weapons by both sides. The development of long-range missiles in the 1950s meant that both the United States and Soviet Union's weapons could reach each other's homelands. By the 1960s, both sides had enough nuclear weapons to destroy their enemy's cities many times over. These weapons were based on planes, submarines and on land. This was to ensure that should one country attack, the other would still have enough missiles left to destroy the enemy country. This theory that no side could win an all-out nuclear war became known as Mutually Assured Destruction (MAD). Many historians feel that it is the key reason why full-scale conflict didn't break out between the two superpowers during the Cold War. The period did, however, see a large-scale arms race between the two sides. By 1981, the United States had 4,000 aircraft and 8,000 long-range missiles that were able to deliver a nuclear weapon. The Soviet Union had similar numbers, all built at a huge cost.

and the Soviet Union spied on one another. They competed fiercely in sports and each tried to be the most dominant power in space exploration.

Soviet soldiers returning from Afghanistan march on a parade. Between 1978 and 1989, the Soviet Union sent over 100,000 troops into Afghanistan to try to prop up the struggling communist government there.

Senator Joseph McCarthy

Joseph Raymond McCarthy studied law and became a judge in the US state of Wisconsin in 1939. He volunteered for the US Marine Corps and flew a number of World War II missions. After the war, he moved into politics and ran a successful yet bitter campaign in 1946 against a fellow Republican Party member, the senator, Robert M. La Follette (Jr).

BORN: 14.11.1908

NATIONALITY: American

PROFESSION: US senator

DIED: 02.05.1957

McCarthy's early years in the US Senate were unremarkable, but in 1950 he became famous when he claimed to have a list of senior government workers who were communists. By this time, fears over communism had grown. This was partly because of news that there were Soviet spies in America, but also because of world events, such as the Soviet Union exploding its first atomic bomb in 1949. That same year, China was taken over by communists led by Mao Zedong.

Many of McCarthy's allegations were proven untrue, but he became head of a powerful Senate committee. This allowed him to continue investigations in an official manner. He made new accusations and the publicity they received led to a number of people losing their jobs or leaving the country. He also accused rival politicians and people in the media of being disloyal to America.

McCarthy asks a question at the 1954 hearings in the US Senate about his investigations. These hearings were broadcast on television and viewed by millions of Americans.

Many were scared of opposing McCarthy for fear of the damage he could do to their careers. However, there was increasing unhappiness with his methods. In 1954, after McCarthy had accused the US Army of harbouring communists, there were thirty-six days of hearings in the Senate. They were televised all over America. The hearings found that one of McCarthy's aides had acted improperly. But it was the bullying and rude manner of McCarthy himself that lost him most of his public and political support. Later in 1954, sixty-seven of the 100 US senators voted to give McCarthy an official warning for the way he had acted. Though McCarthy continued as a senator, his political career was effectively over. He died of an alcohol-related illness two and a half years later.

The cover of an anti-communist comic book first published in 1947. Sensationalist films, posters and books appeared, stoking fears of a communist takeover of America. Some were very popular. This book sold around four million copies.

Reds under the Bed

Russia was a communist nation, and this regime was spreading to many other eastern countries in Europe and Asia during the first years of the Cold War. The United States were alarmed by this. Communists became known as 'Reds', and hysteria over the threat of 'Reds under the Bed' (communists in America) grew in the late 1940s before McCarthy became famous. In 1947, the Federal Employees Loyalty Program was introduced to check on national government workers and their political views. Hundreds lost their jobs as a result. In the same year, the House Committee on Un-American Activities (HCUA) began investigating communism in the movie industry. There were many film-makers, actors, writers and musicians who were accused of communist views or who refused to testify against friends. They were unable to work in Hollywood for many years.

Ethel Rosenberg

Ethel Greenglass was born in New York during World War I. She worked as a clerk and was interested in politics. In the 1930s, she joined the Young Communist League and later, the American Communist Party. Ethel married the engineer Julius Rosenberg in 1939.

BORN: 28.09.1915

NATIONALITY: American

PROFESSION: Spy for the Soviet Union

DIED: 19.06.1953

In 1942, Julius was recruited by the Soviet Union to provide secret engineering information from his workplace. Ethel's brother, David Greenglass, was working on the Manhattan Project to develop an atomic bomb. Greenglass passed on information about the project to the Rosenbergs who, in turn, passed it on to a Soviet agent, Harry Gold.

US and British suspicions about atomic spies persisted after World War II, but it wasn't until 1950 that a major breakthrough occurred. Klaus Fuchs, one of the scientists who worked on the Manhattan Project, was found guilty of spying for the Soviets. He, too, had passed on information to Harry Gold, who was arrested by the FBI. Shortly after, David Greenglass and Ethel and Julius Rosenberg were arrested.

The Rosenbergs' trial began in March 1951. By this time, the anti-communist movement had grown enormously in the United States. Despite doubts about Ethel's role in the spying, both she and her husband were found guilty of espionage. Other members of the Soviet atomic spy ring received long prison sentences.

Ethel Rosenberg sits at her trial, separated from her husband, Julius, by a wire grille. There still remains some doubt over Ethel's precise role in the spy ring.

Harry Gold, for example, was sentenced to thirty years in prison, while Ethel's brother, David Greenglass received fifteen years. Ethel and Julius, however, were sentenced to death, which was a controversial decision. The judge, Irving Kaufman, stated at their trial, 'I consider your crime worse than murder.'

Despite outrage among some in the United States and Europe, the Rosenbergs remained in a New York prison for almost two years. They refused to confess their guilt or to give investigators the names of any others who had been involved in the spy ring.

Ethel and her husband were executed by electric chair on the same day, leaving two sons as orphans. They were the only civilians to be executed for spying by the United States during the Cold War. This has always been a controversial decision and has been attributed to the hysteria over giving away secrets to communists.

Dr Enrico Fermi was a pioneering nuclear physicist who also worked as a consultant on the Manhattan Project. He won the Nobel Prize for physics in 1938, the same year that he emigrated to the United States from his native Italy.

Soviet atomic spies

Tight secrecy surrounded the US atomic bomb project during World War II and in the years afterwards. The United States was confident that the Soviets would not obtain similar technology for a long time. They were shocked when the first Soviet nuclear weapon was tested in 1949. Operation Enormoz had begun during World War II as a Soviet plan to uncover as much about the atomic bomb project as possible. Spies like the Rosenbergs, Theodore Hall, Klaus Fuchs and Morton Sobell passed on atomic secrets, some of which may have helped speeded up the Soviet atomic bomb programme.

Sergei Korolev

The Russian engineer Sergei Korolev (also spelt Korolyov) first began working on rocket engines in the early 1930s while he was working for the government. He designed the Soviet Union's first liquid-fuelled rocket, but was arrested on false charges of sabotage in 1938. He was imprisoned by Stalin in a gulag (prison camp) in Siberia for over five years, and released again in 1944.

BORN: 12.01.1907

NATIONALITY: Russian

PROFESSION: Rocket engineer and pioneer of the Soviet space programme.

DIED: 14.01.1966

When World War II ended, the Soviet Union captured some German scientists and rocket technology. With their input Korolev was ordered to build Soviet versions of the German V2 rocket, but later designed and built his own huge rocket engines. In 1957, Korolev was head of the team which successfully tested the R7 Semyorka in northern Russia. It was the world's first Intercontinental Ballistic Missile (ICBM) – a missile capable of flying more than 5,500 km (3,418 miles). The R7 could fly 7,000 km (4,350 miles), which suddenly meant that all of Europe could be potentially reached by nuclear weapons launched from deep inside the Soviet Union.

The R7 was surpassed quickly as a weapon by other Soviet missile designs, but it became part of the Soviet Union's space programme. Korolev had always hoped that his work would be used peacefully to advance space exploration, and soon after the R7's first launch he got his chance. His team built and launched the world's first satellite, Sputnik, in less than a month. Delighted with the propaganda victory over the United States, the Soviet leader Nikita Kruschev demanded more space successes. Korolev and his team responded with a number of notable firsts. These included Luna 2, which, in 1959, became the first space probe to land on the Moon and two years later, the Vostok programme which made Yuri Gargarin the first man in space.

Korolev poses with a space dog which in 1954 travelled 100 km (62 miles) above Earth onboard a Korolev-designed R1-D rocket. The dog returned to Earth safely.

The space race

The two superpowers competed for supremacy in space after the launch of the Sputnik in 1957. The Soviet Union took an early lead with the first satellite, first probes to Mars and Venus, the first man and first woman in space, as well as the first spacewalk. This stung US pride. The American response was to choose a major mission that would capture public interest. So in a 1961 speech to the US Congress, President Kennedy declared that, by the end of the 1960s, the United States would put a man on the Moon – a feat that was achieved in 1969 with the Apollo 11 mission.

The Vostok 1 spacecraft blasts off from the Baikonur Cosmodrome in 1960. Vostok 1 made Yuri Gargarin the first man in space in 1961. In 1963, Valentina Tereshkova became the first woman in space onboard the Vostok 6.

Despite his many successes, Korolev was always under severe pressure for his position. During his lifetime, he never received the reward and attention his achievements deserved. To the outside world, he was known as the Soviet's Chief Designer. His importance only became widely realised after his death in 1966 when he did not make a recovery following a routine operation.

At the time, Korolev had been working on the N-1 rocket which was to put Soviet men on the Moon.

Gary Powers

Francis Gary Powers was born in Kentucky, USA. After graduating from college, he joined the US Air Force (USAF) in 1950 and trained as a fighter jet pilot. He completed a number of combat missions during the Korean War (1950-53) before being recruited by the Central Intelligence Agency (CIA) – the organisation responsible for most American spying overseas. Powers was sent on aerial spying missions over enemy territory .

BORN: 17.08.1929

NATIONALITY: American

PROFESSION: US spy plane pilot

DIED: 01.08.1977

Powers wears his pilot's pressure suit for flying at high altitude in spy planes like the Lockheed U-2.

On 1 May 1960, Powers took off in a Lockheed U-2 spy plane from an air base in Pakistan. His mission was to secretly photograph Soviet missile bases and land in Bodø in Norway. During the mission, he was detected by Soviet defences that launched aircraft and a salvo of missiles. Powers parachuted to safety but was quickly caught by Soviet forces. His U-2 plane was also recovered. These facts were kept a secret until after the US government issued a statement. It stated that American planes were not spying in Soviet airspace and the downed aircraft was a weather plane that had flown off course.

The Soviets disproved the American claims when they exhibited both Powers and his plane and equipment. They made further propaganda out of Powers' confession that he had been spying. This caused severe embarrassment to the US government. The entire incident heightened the mistrust between the two superpowers. As a result, the United States sped up its work on building unmanned spy satellites.

Eyes in the sky

A U-2 commanded by the US Air Force flies at high altitude above Earth. Over eighty of these aircraft were built and some are still in service over fifty years after their first flight.

Making its first flight in 1955, the Lockheed U-2 was the first near-space observation aircraft of its kind. It could fly at very high altitudes of up to 21,300 metres (69,881 feet). This kept it out of the range of almost all Soviet missiles and aircraft. The U-2 was equipped with state-of-the-art cameras that enabled pilots to take high-resolution images of important locations on the ground. The Lockheed SR-71 Blackbird was developed after Powers was shot down and was first used in 1967. It also flew at high altitudes, but at faster speeds – its maximum speed was over 3,000 km/hr (1,864 mph), more than four times the top speed of the U-2.

Powers was sentenced by the Soviets to ten years in prison, but served less than two. After negotiations between the superpowers, he was exchanged in a spy swap in Berlin for a Soviet agent, Rudolf Abel, in 1962. Returning to the United States, Powers faced an investigation into why he had not managed to destroy the plane or take his own life with his 'dollar of death'. This was a hollowed-out coin containing a lethal poison on a pin that was issued to spy plane pilots. Powers later worked as a test pilot for the aircraft manufacturer Lockheed. From 1970 until his death, he was employed as an airborne weather reporter for American TV stations.

Fidel Castro

A successful lawyer who defended the poor, Castro had also been involved in two attempts to topple the Cuban government. The latter, in 1953, saw him imprisoned for two years for leading a raid on the Moncada army barracks. In 1959, Castro's rebel army managed to oust the military government of General Batista. He was just thirty-two years old when he became leader of Cuba in that same year.

BORN: 13.08.1926

NATIONALITY: Cuban

PROFESSION: Leader of Cuba 1959-2008

Still alive

As Castro secured power in Cuba, over 200,000 Cubans, mainly supporters of the government Castro overthrew, fled. Most of these escaped to

Castro gives a typically passionate speech at a rally between Cuban and Soviet Union leaders in 1963. Castro's annoyance with changes in Soviet policy were tempered by his country's reliance on large amounts of Soviet aid.

the United States where others who joined them later formed a vocal and influential group against Castro's government. Castro visited the United States within months of coming to power to try and impress the media and meet with senior American leaders. But he angered the United States by seizing Cuban land held by American companies. In 1960, Castro made all the American-owned sugar refineries in his country Cuba's property. They responded by refusing to buy Cuba's most important crop, sugar. Later, the United States banned almost all trade with Cuba.

In April 1961, an invasion of Cuba was attempted by around 1,500 Cuban exiles trained and equipped by the CIA. The force landed at the Bay of Pigs, but failed. Most were captured and paraded publicly while Castro made violent speeches against the United States. Secretly, he was concerned about further attempts to depose him, so he sought Soviet help. The Soviet Union supported Castro's communist government and sent aid and troops to Cuba to defend against another invasion. The Soviets also struck an agreement with Castro to place nuclear weapons in Cuba. This led to a huge crisis, known as the

VACATED LAUNCH POSITIONS

MISSILE-READY TENTS

This aerial photograph, taken in November 1962, shows a Soviet missile base being dismantled in Cuba. The missiles and their launching equipment have already gone; they were shipped back to the Soviet Union.

Cuban Missile Crisis, in October 1962 (see panel, below). Despite Castro's fury at the Soviets backing down from the missile crisis, Cuba continued to receive substantial support from the Soviet Union during the 1960s and 1970s. Castro spent some of the aid on improving conditions for the poor by providing free education and health care. However, he also invested in a large military force and sent soldiers and equipment to communist rebel groups around the world including Angola and Bolivia. Castro's rule continued long after the Cold War had ended until 2008, when ill health forced him to hand power over to his brother, Raul.

The Cuban Missile Crisis

The United States had missiles based in Turkey, under 200 km (124 miles) from the Soviet Union border. The Soviets responded in mid-1962 by shipping out large quantities of materials and weaponry to build nuclear missile bases on Cuba, less than 160 km (100 miles) from the American mainland. When US reconnaissance plane photos revealed these bases, a huge stand-off between the two superpowers brought the world closer to nuclear conflict than at any other time during the Cold War. US President Kennedy ordered a blockade, which stopped further Soviet ships reaching Cuba. He also threatened that any use of Soviet nuclear weapons would trigger a huge US nuclear attack in response. Messages flew between Kennedy and the Soviet leader, Nikita Kruschev, before, on 28 October, the Soviets backed down and began removing the missiles.

Võ Nguyên Giáp

In 1931, Võ Nguyên Giáp joined the Indochinese Communist Party in Vietnam. The Communist Party was outlawed in Vietnam in 1939, and many of its members were arrested. Giáp managed to escape to China, but his wife died in prison and his sister-in-law was executed. Giáp joined the guerilla forces of Vietnamese independence leader, Hô Chi Minh and quickly became Hô's trusted deputy.

BORN: 25.08.1911

NATIONALITY: Vietnamese

PROFESSION: North Vietnam general

Still alive

Giáp commanded guerillas fighting the Japanese during World War II and the French forces afterwards. In 1954, his forces secured a famous victory after a fifty-five-day siege of the French forces at Dien Bien Phu, Vietnam. At the Geneva Conference later that year, it was agreed to split Vietnam into two with the French retreating to the south and the communist rebels led by Hô Chi Minh occupying the north. Hô made Giáp Minister of Defence and Commander-in-Chief of the North Vietnamese military.

Giáp was a fierce believer in re-uniting Vietnam by military force, but the US government wanted to contain communism and stop its further spread in Asia. They backed anti-communist governments in South Vietnam and sent increasing amounts of aid, weapons and soldiers. By 1966, over 425,000 American troops were stationed in South Vietnam. Despite facing overwhelming firepower and huge bombing raids on their country, North Vietnamese forces under Giáp's overall command were never fully defeated and managed to draw the war out into a long, bloody struggle.

General Giap was a pioneer of guerrilla warfare. He felt the only way North Vietnam could win was to keep its enemy occupied in a long, drawn-out struggle.

South Vietnamese forces patrol a trail in the neighbouring country of Laos during the Vietnam War. Giap's troops often used jungle trails in Laos and isolated parts of Vietnam to send down supplies, weapons and reinforcements.

In 1968, Giáp abandoned the previous strategy of guerrilla warfare in favour of an all-out attack in open battle. Called the Tet Offensive, Giáp's gamble failed, with his forces beaten back and large losses. But it was a point in the conflict at which many Americans began to think that the war was not winnable. Powerful protests for peace sprung up in the United States and by the spring of 1973, US troops had left Vietnam. Giáp and other generals commanded the North Vietnamese army, which advanced through South Vietnam capturing the capital city of Saigon in April 1975. The following year, Vietnam became a single, independent country.

Containment

Throughout much of the Cold War, the United States practised a foreign policy known as Containment. This involved stopping communism spreading any further around the world by providing large amounts of support to friendly or anti-communist governments. This policy led the United States to offer substantial aid and support to the anti-communist South Vietnamese government in its struggle against communist North Vietnam. As the Vietnam War progressed, the US escalated its involvement in the war, sending hundreds of thousands of troops and vast amounts of weaponry. North Vietnam received aid from a small number of other communist nations, most notably China, while the Soviet Union sent few troops or technicians but larger amounts of arms and equipment.

Yuri Andropov

The son of a railway worker, Yuri Vladimirovich Andropov joined the Soviet Communist Party in 1939. In 1954, he was appointed Soviet ambassador to Hungary, one of the countries of eastern Europe under communist control and loyal to the Soviet Union. Two years later, Andropov was a major influence in the Soviet Union's decision to invade and suppress the Hungarian revolt in 1956 (see panel, right).

BORN: 15.06.1914

NATIONALITY: Russian

PROFESSION: Head of the KGB (1967-82)
Soviet leader (1982-84)

DIED: 09.02.1984

In 1967, Andropov was made head of the powerful Soviet intelligence agency, the KGB. The KGB had a huge budget and vast powers to spy on people both inside and outside the Soviet Union. It also acted as a secret police force with powers to suppress any critics inside the country. At its peak under Andropov, it is estimated that the KGB employed some 480,000 people including 200,000 border guards. Thousands of people were investigated by the KGB and arrested and imprisoned in prison camps.

Andropov proved a ruthless head of the KGB and used his influence to insist on an invasion of Czechoslovakia in 1968. In a period known as the Prague Spring, Czechoslovakia had begun making many reforms that angered the Soviets. He was also influential in the decision to send large numbers of Soviet troops into Afghanistan in 1979 when the communist government there was under threat. This dragged the Soviet Union into a long, costly war against the Afghan Mujahideen rebels that lasted a decade.

Yuri Andropov was a powerful figure in Soviet politics for much of the Cold War period, first as a diplomat, then as KGB head and finally, Soviet leader.

Andropov was promoted in 1973 to become a full member of the highest level of government in the Soviet Union, the Politburo, while remaining head of the KGB. In November 1982, after the death of Leonid Breshnev, he was made Soviet leader. In his short period in charge, Andropov suffered from ill health. Although he tried to tackle corruption, he achieved little more than increasing tension with the United States. One of his most important decisions as leader was the choice of Mikhail Gorbachev as his deputy (see page 26).

A Soviet tank rolls into Prague, the capital city of Czechoslovakia in August 1968. Some 200,000 troops and 2,000 tanks from the Soviet Union, Hungary, Poland and Bulgaria put an end to the Prague Spring.

Hungarian revolt

In 1956, Hungary became a hotbed of revolt with widespread anti-Soviet demonstrations. The country's new prime minister, Imre Nagy, began to abolish communist regulations, gave Hungarians freedom of speech and then announced Hungary would leave the Warsaw Pact. The Soviet reaction, urged on by Andropov, was swift and brutal. Masses of Soviet tanks rolled into Hungary, killing at least 4,000 people, while around 200,000 more fled the country. Imre Nagy was arrested and later executed. His replacement was Janos Kadar who was loyal to the Soviet Union. The Soviets kept a troop presence in Hungary for over thirty years.

Anwar el-Sādāt

After plotting to rid Egypt of the British during World War II, Muhammad Anwar el-Sādāt joined the Free Officers organisation. The political party came to power in a military coup in 1952. As a trusted aide to President Gamar Nasser, Sādāt held many senior government positions in the next 20 years, including Vice-President of Egypt from 1964 to 1970. Nasser made Egypt one of the major leaders of a country that was not allied to either superpower, but sometimes sought aid from both sides.

BORN: 25.12.1918

NATIONALITY: Egyptian

PROFESSION: President of Egypt (1970-1981)

DIED: 06.10.1981

After the Suez Crisis in 1956, Nasser forged closer links with the Soviet Union. When Nasser died in 1970 and Sādāt became President, it was assumed that he would follow suit. Sādāt, however, made major changes. He dismissed many members of Nasser's government and, in 1972, expelled hundreds of Soviet advisors and technical support staff from his country. After his links with the Soviet Union weakened, Sādāt forged closer ties with the United States later in the 1970s. This angered many in the Arab world. For a period, though, Sādāt was considered a military hero both in Egypt and in many Arab nations. In 1973, he established Egypt as a military force by fighting the Arab-Israeli war along with Syria. Although the conflict ended largely in stalemate, it was seen by many as an Egyptian victory and proof that Egypt was a strong nation.

Sādāt embraces former US President, Richard Nixon at the funeral of Iranian leader, Mohammad Reza Pahlavi. Sādāt's moves to improve relations with the United States angered some in Egypt.

Sādāt shocked the Arab world in 1977 by becoming the first Arab leader to visit Israel's capital, Jerusalem. In 1978, this was followed by lengthy peace negotiations with Israel, during which Sādāt and Israeli prime minister Menachem Begin signed a number of pledges. The pair signed a full peace treaty in 1979. Sādāt's popularity was high, especially with the

Arab-Israeli wars

Both superpowers vied to gain a say in the Middle East, the world's most crucial region for oil production. While the United States was Israel's key ally and the Soviet Union supplied large amounts of aid to Egypt and other Arab nations, both superpowers found it hard to exert much influence and were unable to prevent a series of wars that broke out in the region. Israel had captured much territory during the 1967 Six Day War, gaining the West Bank from Jordan's control, the Golan Heights from Syria and the Sinai Peninsula and Gaza Strip from Egypt. The United Nations issued repeated calls for Israel to withdraw from these areas but Israel refused. In October 1973, Egypt and Syria launched major attacks at the same time to retake the territory from Israel. After great advances by its enemies, Israel repelled the attacks and its troops advanced into Egyptian and Syrian territory. The war ended in stalemate, but later peace agreements led to some of the land being returned by Israel.

United States and its allies and he and Begin received the Nobel Peace Prize in 1978. At home, however, the economy was struggling and there were riots and demonstrations. Sādāt had angered many who did not want peace with Israel.

In 1979, Egypt was expelled from the Arab League – an organisation of North African and Middle Eastern countries. Two years later, while watching a military parade in Cairo that commemorated the 1973 Arab-Israeli war, Sādāt was assassinated by Muslim extremists.

Anwar Sādāt (left), Jimmy Carter, and Menachem Begin sign the historic agreement between Israel and Egypt known as the Camp David Accord in Washington DC in 1978.

Lech Wałęsa

Born in Popowo in Poland, Lech Wałęsa worked as an electrician in his home town. In 1967, he moved to find work at the gigantic Lenin Shipyard in the Polish port of Gdansk. During the 1970s, he organised trade union activity in the shipyards, which was against the law at the time.

In 1976, Wałęsa lost his job due to his union activities. He earned his livelihood by taking on temporary jobs, but also tried to organise unions alongside Poland's coastal areas. But in 1980, when Gdansk shipyard workers protested at rising prices of meat, he climbed over the shipyard fence to join them. He was made head of the strike committee. Instead of just pressing for higher wages, Wałęsa campaigned for greater rights, including the right for workers to strike and to organise their own union.

From this strike committee grew Poland's first labour union – Solidarity (see panel, right). Within months, ten million Poles had joined it or formed similar unions. These great changes were halted when General Wojciech Jaruzelski came to power in Poland in late 1981. He tried to crush Solidarity by banning its activities and arresting many of its leading members, including Wałęsa.

After eleven months under house arrest near the Poland-Soviet border, Wałęsa was released, but his every move was followed by Polish secret police. He still managed to maintain contact with Solidarity. The union had gone underground and secretly organised further strikes and protests.

BORN: 29.09.1943

NATIONALITY: Polish

PROFESSION: Shipworker Leader of Solidarity trade union.

Still alive

Lech Wałęsa attends an early rally of the Polish trade union, Solidarity. In 1978, he had become active in secret unions based on the coast of Poland.

Wałęsa leads a march on the anniversary of Solidarity's founding. The union believed in non-violent protests and gained much support from various left wing groups, as well as the Catholic Church.

In 1983, he won the Nobel Peace Prize but sent his wife, Danuta, to Sweden to collect the award as he feared the communist Polish government would not allow him back into his home country.

By the late 1980s, the Soviet government, led by Mikhail Gorbachev, had made it clear that communist governments in eastern Europe would have to support themselves and not look to the Soviet Union for help. Poland's economy and government was struggling. So when Wałęsa organised another major strike at the dockyards in 1988, General Jaruzelski entered talks with Solidarity. The result was the first elections in which non-communists could stand for over half a century.

In 1989, Wałęsa helped a fellow member of Solidarity, Tadeusz Mazowiecki, become Prime Minister of Poland, but Wałęsa beat Mazowiecki in the 1990 election to become Poland's President. He helped guide the country through its first free elections for parliament but his plain-speaking, confrontational style proved unpopular with many Polish people and he failed to be re-elected as president in 1995.

Solidarity

Formed in 1980, Solidarnosc (meaning Solidarity) grew out of the Workers' Defence Committee – a group started in Poland in 1976 to help support the families of striking workers who were imprisoned. Solidarity was the first non-communist trade union in a communist country. It pressed hard for improved rights for workers and and its supporters took part in peaceful strikes and demonstrations, rather than violence, to campaign for change. Solidarity's survival and success was a major inspiration to trade union and anti-communist movements in other eastern European countries.

Aldrich Ames

During the Cold War, both sides worked hard to recruit spies with important knowledge of the enemy's military, political plans and spy services. The US spy Aldrich Hazen Ames was one of the Soviet KGB's most notable successes, and he was also the highest paid spy in history.

BORN: 26.05.1941

NATIONALITY: American

PROFESSION: CIA officer who spied for the Soviet Union

Still alive

Ames stands in handcuffs at his trial for conspiracy to commit espionage. His intelligence proved extremely damaging to the CIA as it allowed the Soviet Union and, later, Russia, to pinpoint security breaches.

Ames was the son of a CIA officer. His first mission abroad was to Turkey in 1969 to try to recruit Soviet intelligence workers to work for the United States. Ames was promoted a number of times and ended up working as the head of the CIA's Soviet Counterintelligence Division. In this highly sensitive role, he knew the identities of most, if not all, of the spies inside the Soviet Union working for America.

By 1985, Ames was in the middle of a divorce and deep in debt. He contacted the Soviet Embassy in Washington and offered secrets for money. Over the next nine years, he revealed details of over ninety US missions or military operations and the identities of as many as twenty-five to thirty valuable spies. One of the first to be betrayed was also one of the most important. General Dmitri Polyakov (codenamed Top Hat) was a senior officer in Soviet military intelligence. He had been passing top secret information on Soviet weapons to the Americans since 1961, but following Ames' betrayal, was arrested in 1986. Two years later he was executed. Suspicions started to mount as more and more US spies were captured and silenced.

The CIA conducted investigations without ever identifying the source of the leaks. This was surprising, as Ames was paid a modest salary by the CIA, but lived a luxurious lifestyle with a large house and expensive car. He was ordered to sit two polygraph (lie detector) tests – the first in 1986, the second in 1991.

He passed both and was allowed to continue working. By this time, the Soviet Union had broken up but Ames continued working for Russia.

In February 1994, Ames and his second wife, Rosario, were arrested shortly before flying to Moscow. He pleaded guilty to all charges of espionage (spying). In April 1994, he was sentenced to life imprisonment with no possibility of release. He had been paid over four million US dollars by the Soviets, two million of which remain in an unknown bank account.

West German leader Willy Brandt (left) attends an election meeting with his trusted aide Günter Guillaume (right), who turned out to be a long-time spy for East German intelligence.

German spies

Günter Guillaume was a sleeper – an agent who is put in place by one side but may not start spying for many years. Guillaume was a sleeper for the East German intelligence service, the Stasi. Under their orders, he had moved to West Germany from East Germany in 1956 and built a career as a successful young politician. In 1970 he was appointed an advisor to the West German Chancellor, Willy Brandt. Guillaume sat in on crucial top level meetings, read Brandt's confidential messages with world leaders and gained access to vital military and economic reports. He passed all of this information on to the Stasi. When he was discovered in 1974, it provoked a scandal and Brandt resigned as West German leader.

Mikhail Gorbachev

At school, Mikhail Gorbachev was considered one of the most intelligent pupils and he graduated with a silver medal in 1950. He then went on to study law at Moscow State University. He gradually rose through the ranks of the Communist Party that controlled the Soviet Union. For over twenty years, he lived and worked in his home region of Stavropol, where he earned a reputation as an honest and hardworking party official.

BORN: 02.03.1931

NATIONALITY: Russian

PROFESSION: President of the Soviet Union (1985–91)

Still alive

Gorbachev talks to people from the Lithuanian city of Vilnius. Previous Soviet leaders were very remote, but Gorbachev tried to meet ordinary people. His charm and charisma impressed many.

Stavropol was far from the centre of power at Moscow. Fortunately, Gorbachev had several powerful mentors, including Yuri Andropov (see page 18). In 1980, he became the youngest full member of the inner circle of Soviet government, the Politburo.

Gorbachev became the Soviet Union's leader in 1985 and worked hard to tackle the economic problems the country was facing. He promoted many younger staff to key positions, tried to combat corruption and attempted to update the Soviet's declining industries. He secured agreements with the United States for both sides to reduce their numbers of nuclear weapons, began to withdraw Soviet forces from eastern European countries and ended the Afghanistan war in 1989. All of these moves were designed to cut back the enormous sums of money spent by the country on the military and aid and support to other communist nations.

Gorbachev answered the growing number of calls for reform at home with many changes.

In 1987, Gorbachev (left, with 40th US President Reagan) signed the Intermediate-Range Nuclear Forces (INF) Treaty which banned a major class of nuclear weapons. This was followed by the 1991 START treaty which saw both sides destroy several thousand nuclear weapons each.

Glasnost and perestroika

Two of Gorbachev's most important policies became well-known words all over the world. Perestroika means 'restructuring' and ensured that the power of government over businesses was reduced. For the first time in decades, ordinary Soviet people were allowed to own and run businesses. Glasnost means 'openness' and gave the media more freedoms and allowed ordinary people to criticise and debate government policies. The impact of glasnost and perestroika quickly spread to other communist countries in eastern Europe.

These included allowing more freedom of speech and eventually enabling other political parties to run for power besides the Communist Party. He was hailed as a man of peace abroad and was awarded the Nobel Peace Prize in 1990. But his reforms earned him many enemies at home.

He clashed repeatedly with many in the military and Communist Party who did not want change and blocked a number of his policies. In August 1991, attempts to remove him in a coup while he was on holiday failed. Yet, by this time, independence movements had sprung up all over the Soviet Union and in the nations of communist eastern Europe. Gorbachev's time in power only lasted until the end of December 1991, when he resigned as leader and the Soviet Union officially broke up into fifteen separate republics. Gorbachev is still active in politics to this day. In 2008, he formed the Independent Democratic Party of Russia with former head of the KGB, Alexander Lebedev and in 2009 met with US President, Barack Obama.

Cold War movies

At the Cold War's start, fear of communism began to build quickly in the United States. Some movie studios sought to reflect this with films that were patriotic and showed communists as evil doers. Some featured sensational titles and themes such as *The Red Menace* and *Invasion USA*. In 1949, RKO Studios released *I Married A Communist*, starring Robert Ryan. Thirteen directors refused to make the film and public reaction to the movie's title was very negative.

Early 1950s films such as *Big Jim McLain* (starring John Wayne), *Kiss Me Deadly* and *Security Risk* were more successful. They tended to give the impression that the US was overrun with communist spies and helped reinforce public fears.

By the mid-1950s, the American people were more concerned with communism in the Soviet Union and the fears of nuclear weapons and radiation. Science fiction films of the decade like *Them!* and *The Beginning of the End* portrayed scary mutant creatures created by radioactivity. By this time, both sides had built long-range missiles with nuclear warheads capable of reaching the heart of the enemy's country. It was, therefore, inevitable that some films looked at the possibility of nuclear war between the two superpowers. These included Stanley Kramer's *On the Beach* (1959) and the 1964 movies, *Fail-Safe* and *Dr Strangelove*.

Films released in the 1970s and 1980s, including *The Falcon and the Snowman*, were critical of America and its conduct. Others, such as *Red Dawn* and *World War III*, returned to the themes of a Soviet Union attack on America, or in the cases of *War Games* and *The Manhattan Project*, the continuing fear of nuclear warfare.

Dr Strangelove was a dark comedy starring Peter Sellers, who played three different characters in the film. It was one of a handful of movies that explored the risks of having nuclear weapons and whether all-out nuclear war could be triggered by a mistake or by a rogue general or politician.

A scene from the film *I Married A Communist* that was later re-released under the new title *The Woman on Pier 13*.

Spy shows and films

The public fascination with spies and spying boomed in the 1960s with many TV shows like *Get Smart*, *The Man From UNCLE* and the first James Bond films. They portrayed the world of spying as exciting and glamorous. But some movies, including *The Spy Who Came In From The Cold* and *The Ipcress File*, painted a darker, and more realistic picture, of spying as a deadly and dangerous activity with both sides guilty of brutal killings.

Read It, See It, Hear It

Here are some website links that will help you explore films from the Cold War era further:

http://www.filmsite.org/thrillerfilms3.html
Read about James Bond and other fictional spies featured in films and books during the Cold War.

http://www.russiankafe.com/2007/03/16/cold-war-films/
Watch some clips and trailers of movies made during the Cold War.

http://history.sandiego.edu/gen/filmnotes/drstrangelove.html
Learn more about the making of the film whose full title was *Dr Strangelove, or: How I Learned to Stop Worrying and Love the Bomb.*

http://www.lib.berkeley.edu/MRC/Warfilm.html
Scroll down to read short summaries of a number of famous movies during the Cold War period.

Timeline: Cold War

People | ## Events

1945
End of World War II.

1949
Formation of the North Atlantic Treaty Organisation (NATO).
First Soviet nuclear weapons tested.

1950
McCarthy begins his allegations and investigations into communists in the US government and armed forces.

1953
Ethel and Julius Rosenberg executed. Other atomic spies sentenced to imprisonment.

1954
KGB formed in the same year that the CIA helps overthrow unfriendly governments in Guatemala and Iran.

1957
Soviet rocket engineers led by Sergei Korolev produce the first long range rocket missile and the first satellite.

1959
Fidel Castro seizes power in Cuba.

1959
The Suez Crisis over the nationalisation of the Suez Canal.

1962
The Cuban Missile Crisis leads to heightened tension between US and Soviet Unions over nuclear missiles based on the island of Cuba.

1967
Yuri Andropov made head of the KGB, the Soviet intelligence agency.

1968
Soviet troops crush the revolt in Czechoslovakia.

1970
Anwar el-Sādāt becomes President of Egypt.

1973
Egypt and Syria attack Israel in the Arab-Israeli War. Peace agreed the following year.

1979
Anwar el-Sādāt and Menachem Begin sign an historic Israeli-Egyptian peace agreement.

1980
Solidarity trades union formed in Poland and gains millions of members.

1985
Mikhail Gorbachev becomes leader of the Soviet Union and begins making reforms.

1991
Soviet Union splits into Russia and fourteen other independent republics.

Glossary

aid financial or other forms of assistance given to one group or country by another.

arms race a massive military build-up by two or more rivals or enemies. During the Cold War, the Soviet Union and the United States both engaged in a huge arms race to gain military superiority.

civil war a war between opposing groups within one country.

depose to remove someone from a position of power.

Geneva Conference a formal meeting between many countries held in 1954 with the aim of restoring peace in Vietnam and French Indochina.

Guerrillas people who fight in a group that fights an enemy by ambushes and surprise hit-and-run attacks.

Intercontinental Ballistic Missile (ICBM) a type of missile capable of travelling long distances, such as between continents.

Mutually Assured Destruction (MAD) the idea that if one superpower launched a large nuclear attack, the other would be able to do the same, ensuring that both countries would be destroyed.

mentors people who help and advise others usually in the same field of work.

North Atlantic Treaty Organisation (NATO) a military alliance featuring the United States and its allies.

Politburo the top level of government in the Soviet Union during the Cold War.

propaganda spreading a particular message to try to influence public opinion or make people perform certain actions.

reforms changes designed to improve something.

superpower a powerful nation economically and militarily which plays a leading role in the world. During the Cold War, the United States and Soviet Union were the world's two superpowers.

suppress to forcibly put an end to something, such as a protest.

trade union an organisation of workers that campaigns for improvements in their members' working conditions.

United Nations (UN) An organisation set up after World War II with the aim of helping countries to sort out disputes without fighting.

Warsaw Pact A military alliance of the Soviet Union and its allies in Eastern Europe, set up in 1955.

Further information

Books To Read
How Did It Happen?: The Cold War, Paul Harrison, Franklin Watts, 2007.

Questioning History: the Arab-Israeli Conflict, Cath Senker, Wayland, 2008

Spies and Spying, Clive Gifford, Oxford University Press, 2009.

Fidel Castro, Ellen R. Butts and Joyce R. Schwarz, Lerner, 2006.

Leading Lives: *Mikhail Gorbachev*, David Downing, Heinemann Library, 2004.

Places To Visit
The National Cold War Exhibition
RAF Cosford Museum, Shifnal, Shropshire, TF11 8UP, UK
Website: http://www.nationalcoldwarexhibition.org.uk

The Stasi Museum
Forschungs- und Gedenkstätte
Normannenstr. Ruschestr. 103, Haus 1
10365 Berlin
Website: http://www.stasimuseum.de/en/enausstellung.htm

International Spy Museum
800 F Street, NW Washington, DC 20004 USA.
Website: http://www.spymuseum.org/

Websites
http://www.coldwar.org/
An excellent in-depth website looking at different aspects of the Cold War with features on the Rosenbergs, Joseph McCarthy, Yuri Andropov and many more, all searchable by decade.

http://www.bbc.co.uk/history/worldwars/coldwar/
The BBC's Cold War webpages have great features on the Cuban Missile Crisis, the fall of the Soviet Union, amongst others.

http://www.pbs.org/wgbh/nova/venona/
Read and learn more about the atomic spies during the Cold War at this interesting Public Broadcasting Service website.

http://www.learningcurve.gov.uk/coldwar
An interesting website with worksheets and documents about the Cold War and important debates and turning points.

http://www.fbi.gov/libref/historic/famcases/ames/ames.htm
Read a brief FBI report on the case of Aldrich Ames.

Index

THE WHO'S WHO OF...

CONTENTS OF TITLES IN THE SERIES: